Insider's Guide to

Scrapping, Junking & Generating FAST Cash

Diana Loera

Table of Contents

Additional Books by Diana Loera

Summertime Sangria

Best Copycat Recipes on the Planet

Party Time Chicken Wing Recipes

Awesome Thanksgiving Leftovers Revive Guide

Best Venison Recipes

Meet Me at the County Fair – Fair Food Recipes

What is the Paleo Diet & Paleo Diet Recipe Sampler

12 Extra Special Summer Dessert Fondue Recipes

14 Extra Special Winter Holidays Fondue Recipes

USA Based Wholesale Directory 2014

Fast Start Guide to Flea Market Selling

I601A – Our Journey to Ciudad Juarez

Stop Hot Flashes Now

Please visit www.LoeraPublishing.com to view all titles and descriptions. Thank you.

Note from the Author

Hello! Diana Loera here.

I'll be your guide in this book and will be sharing with you the ins and outs of scrapping and junking.

I'm a long time marketer and an author.

I've also learned, firsthand, that it is easy to generate fast cash- if you have the right plan.

I was researching a project about four years ago for an infomercial idea.

The project idea was surviving in a down economy and I was looking for opportunities to share on TV with others in an infomercial.

Needless to say, as the "mark up" of an infomercial product has to be quite high to cover costs to produce the infomercial and advertise – this book would have been priced a lot higher than it is today if it was part of an infomercial program. I do my best to keep book costs down but I also want to provide photos as my readers say they prefer to have photos included if possible.

The infomercial project led me on a very interesting path.

I opened a flea market booth and have done very well especially when you consider the small amount of time invested weekly.

I compiled a wealth of wholesale sources along the way,

I did some online freelancing and made over $8,000 in a few short months working -at most- 1 hour every few days.

I really can't call what I did as "work" either since I don't wake up to an alarm and I pretty much make my own schedule – as the saying goes, no boss, no phone, no problems.

Now I've decided to reveal one more fast way to make money fast – money as in hard, cold cash.

By the way – if any of the topics I just mentioned caught your attention, yes I created books on these topics, inexpensively priced so others could duplicate my successful actions, get shortcuts and learn my secrets that allowed me to generate cash fast.

You may wonder why on earth I would be so willing to tell people my fast cash earning secrets and the answer is simple. I believe that there is always enough to go around.

Sure, telling you about scrapping and junking is going to result in more scrappers and junkers but I believe in helping others and that the more we help each other, the more there is to go around.

That may sound corny but it is the best way that I can explain my thought process on the topic.

You'll find that I write as though we are talking together over coffee at a local diner.

I answer my emails – so if you read this book and have some questions or want to share your scrapping stories, at the end of this book is my email address.

I'm an average person. I made good money when the economy was good and when people bought infomercial products on TV.

But with the changing economy came changes in the infomercial business. I found it to be perfect timing that I was researching ways to make cash in a down economy when the infomercial business started changing.

Those changes have allowed me to focus more and more on writing and finding cool and helpful topics like the one you are reading about now.

So, enough about me. Let's get moving to the real reason you have read this far – HOW TO MAKE FAST CASH (and have fun too).

Introduction

Maybe you've seen the vehicles driving through your neighborhood on garbage day –

No, we aren't referring to garbage trucks.

We're talking about scrappers and junkers – people who drive through neighborhoods and collect scrap metal and curbside finds.

With the economy going from bad to worse, average families are now looking at ways to stretch every cent.

Senior citizens also get in on the game and are able to add a nice supplement to their fixed income.

People of all ages are taking a closer look at what is sitting on the curb each week. Are you ready to get in on what may be an incredible opportunity?

While everyone would like more cash in their pocket at the end of each week, working a second job often isn't realistic.

First of all, is there a job to be found? The second problem is – does the second job hours work with the first job hours and any school or family events?

Scrapping and junking is something that almost anyone can do. There are some things you will need such as a reliable vehicle but I've seen people scrap and junk on a smaller scale on foot and on bicycles.

This past summer, I watched a guy in his early 20's accumulate a decent amount of scrap during the month of July. He doesn't have a car and found the scrap by walking or riding his bike on streets near his home. It was enough to cover his expenses for several days at the county fair which was something that was out of his budget otherwise.

I know a fellow scrapper who told me that quite simply, the cost of living has hurt him financially. He scraps after work as the extra money helps with his bills and he is not tied down to a set second job.

I also know people who scrap full time and are able to pay monthly bills by doing so.

What it comes down to is that if you need cash income, scrapping and junking may be worth considering.

In this book you'll learn about scrapping and junking plus some insider tips.

I'm a numbers person. I work with numbers a lot with advertising and I work with ROI – Return on Investment.

So I started thinking about how many washers equaled how much money and what one could make on average each day scrapping.

Then I started researching different cities and towns in the area, their trash pick -up days, their ordinances regarding scrapping

We then began scrapping using the strategy that I have outlined in this book.

I published this book in a larger size 8 ½ by 11 as I personally hate trying to read a small book with tiny print. I am in the process of publishing this book in large print format also.

So with this being said – let's keep moving and see if one or more of the strategies in this book is one that will work for you.

The best thing is – you can start immediately.

Like any smart business person, you do need to have some discipline and work this like a business if you want to have the best results.

In this book we're going to walk through the overall process, the do's and don'ts, the tips and the strategy that I know, with certainty, works.

This book is a beginner's guide. If you are already scrapping and making tons of money, then no, this book isn't for you. If you're scrapping and think you've got a strategy that works just fine, then no, this book isn't for you.

We are also going to cover junking and ways to generate cash from both scrapping and junking.

To clarify for this book – scrapping refers to the collection of metal scrap.

Junking refers to the collection of non- metal items or sometimes metal items that can be resold if cleaned up and/or repaired.

I have seen the words scrapping and junking interchanged depending upon the region of the US so before we started this book I wanted to ensure that you, the reader, understood my definition of scrapping and junking.

If you are looking for ways to make extra money, possibly without leaving your regular job and/or you just want to supplement your income short term then this book may be helpful.

If you've lost your job or feel you're stuck in a dead end job with no hope of a raise, this book may give you some ideas to help add income.

This book was created to help you get a jump start on making money fast.

We will not be going over current payouts for various types of metal in this book.

Metal prices change frequently and also vary by regions.

We will discuss how to maximize your profits by researching the best payouts in your area.

We are also going to take a very realistic look at scrapping and junking.

You'll get the insider's viewpoint and also insider tips regarding how to maximize your income potential.

I like to say this is a business where you just need to work smarter, not necessarily harder, to see a decent cash flow.

I have seen countless people jump in their vehicle, drive around and fizzle out. Some don't even last an hour, some last a week or so and then give up.

If you do not like driving, this opportunity may not be a good fit for you.

If you do not like getting dirty – pass on this idea.

Then we have what is rather humbling – no matter how much money that you have in the bank, or how many cars you have, or what your day job, some people have a preconceived idea of scrappers that is just not good.

I'm a professional, college educated, business woman. My husband has owned a successful business and also was a police officer. Yet, in some cases, I have watched people talk to us like we are vagrants. You must let this roll off of you. If I had to give you only one tip- this may be the one that I would choose.

I have seen an insane amount of people show up at a scrap yard proudly driving their almost new truck with scrap metal scratching up the bed or, and I really don't know which is worse, a late model truck pulling a trailer and on it one washer. These people show up usually for one of two reasons – they do not want a scrapper to get this item which usually is worth all of $10 scrap, before gas and time or they saw an ad that the scrap yard pays "good" money and they think they will make a bundle of cash from one sink, one washer, one dryer etc.. These types never come back again.

I've also seen a well -dressed man driving a late model Jaguar come to the scrap yard to bring in a pair of used brake rotors. I'm not sure why someone driving a car like his would take the time to bring in two small pieces of metal but maybe penny pinching is how he got the Jag.

But I'm not done yet – I watched two well -dressed middle aged women coming rolling in to a scrap yard and loudly announce to the worker in the yard (while 6 scrappers were unloading their trucks right next to these two gems) that they were delivering their two metal folding chairs as they "didn't want to put them on the curb for THOSE scrap people to take". Alrighty then……

I've watched a man in a very affluent neighborhood come running out of his house, screeching like a banshee when metal was picked up from his curb. Metal that was propped up right alongside his garbage cans but he took offense to someone stopping to pick it up.

I've watched women totally disregard that their children were playing and running into the street. A scrapper had to come to a full stop and wait several minutes for the children to clear from the middle of the street. Neither woman did anything to move the children or reprimand them. Personally, I think their actions were intentional.Yet another day, the same two women shouted at a scrapper to slow down when their children were not outside – the scrapper was going 15 miles UNDER the speed limit. I know as I was in the truck.

But to match those bad experiences are many, many good experience and I would like to say the good outweighs the bad but you need to expect both.

It has taken me a good amount of restraint numerous times not to tell the ones with attitude that I was writing a book on scrapping and that they would definitely be included as examples.

I've watched a man from another affluent neighborhood come outside and flag down a scrapper as the man had remodeled his kitchen and had several appliances to be hauled away. He helped the scrapper load the appliances and said come back same time next week, there would be more metal on the curb – needless to say, there was. He waves at the scrapper any time he happens to be outside when the scrapper is driving by.

I've seen another man flag down a scrapper and give him a like new mower because he just bought a new one.

On the flip side – I've seen scrappers destroy bags of garbage. I've seen boxes ripped open and stuff strewn on the curb – by scrappers. This is NOT okay and it results in problems.

I've watched scrappers lift the lids off garbage cans and forage through bags of garbage- just not cool and definitely something you should not do.

I've also read in the newspapers about people who call themselves scrappers being arrested for stealing copper and other metals. These are not scrappers – these are thieves.

Dealing with Problem People

You will most likely cross paths with at least one person, scrapper or not who has serious issues.

I do not advise EVER getting out of your vehicle or participating in their name calling.

These clowns go from just dimwits to dangerous. You don't know what you may be dealing with and I advise you to always keep a mobile in your vehicle.

As mentioned, do not get out and attempt to reason or confront.

It is best to drive away. If they follow you then head towards a well -lit public area, even better yet, a police station.

To give you just a few examples of dimwit to dangerous –

People, usually men, who flag you down and then act like they didn't when you loop back to see what they wanted. This is a weird game that I have yet to figure out. Often they have a neighbor or friend with them. The bad thing is – normal people may also wave as they have an item so it makes sense to loop back. Just keep moving if they then claim that no they didn't wave. No sense arguing with them.

People who think they are traffic cops. These people, mostly men but I've seen a few women to this also – you can be going 10 miles UNDER the posted speed limit and they will start shouting and screaming at you to slow down.

You can't win with these people. I find it is best to open my window and say I'm sorry, what did you say? BUT you must say this in a very nice and friendly manner. They usually settle down a little and then they repeat themselves. No matter how slow we have been going, I then reply, again extremely nicely – ahhhh, okay, thank you for letting me know or something along that line. It usually takes them back. But then you must move on – immediately.

Worst case that we have experienced thus far – at night – dark subdivision – all of a sudden this very large red pickup comes barreling at us. We had been in a cul de sac and he tried to block us in. It was scary. We pulled around him and he rolled down his window. It was evident to me this guy was most likely inebriated. He shouted at us to slow down.

In looking back, I think not responding may have resulted in him ramming us or worst.

I looked up at him and very pleasantly and evenly toned said thank you for letting us know. We then drove away. I can't guarantee you will have the same outcome but in this case I knew I had to acknowledge him and I also knew we had to get away from him – fast.

I think he expected a confrontation and the couple moments that it took him to process the response and think about what to do next, gave us the opening to calmly drive away.

Second worst was actually a confrontation with another scrapper. We had not seen him in that neighborhood before. He pulled up alongside us and he had a boy, I'm guessing possibly his son, riding with him. The boy was maybe ten years old.

The man announces to us that the bike we had picked up – he must have seen us pick it up – was actually being held for his son. He went on to say that the homeowner had told him he could have it and went to get his truck.

I know a lie when I hear it and this guy was lying through his teeth plus the homeowner had talked with us a few minutes before and helped us load the bike and some other items. I said something to the effect of I'm sorry, I think you've mistaken us for someone else, I don't think that was the case and we started to drive away. The scrapper then called me every foul name you could think of.

My husband then backed up the truck.

Whereas, I would advise you to have kept driving and ignore the lunatic, my husband took huge offense to his wife being called a variety of names.

The scrapper then began calling my husband a selection of racial slurs peppered with swear words while the son laughed.

My husband said later, he could see in the guy's truck and the guy had a baseball bat on his lap. This guy was looking for trouble. We drove off and we saw the scrapper only one time after during that season – he turned and went the other way.

Looking back what bothers me the most is that the child was so calm and laughed during the ordeal.

While most fellow scrappers will wave when you pass, some will flip you off. Don't do the same, it is just not worth it.

We have had some try to block us, one tell my husband that this was "his area" and countless ones speed up and floor it to pass us in a subdivision. Ignore them and continue on.

I could share with you hundreds of stories as I've seen just about every scenario imaginable at the scrap yards and while scrapping.

Soon enough though you'll have your own collection of stories.

I make a point of including these stories so you go into this opportunity with eyes wide open.

No one gave me the guided tour first and we learned the hard way.

Most time it was a good learning experience but sometimes there were some scary moments like the couple I just shared with you.

I'd rather prepare you as much as possible in advance and that is the purpose of my stories.

A Simple Guide to Scrap

When you go to the scrap yard you will most likely see the phrases ferrous scrap metal and non -ferrous scrap metal.

I think one of the most common questions is – what is the difference between the two?

The technical answer is -

Ferrous metals and alloys contain iron and non-ferrous materials do not.

Sounds fairly simple doesn't it?

But how do you know the difference between the two?

Ferrous metals include mild steel, carbon steel, stainless steel, cast iron, and wrought iron.

It is a good rule of thumb that if you see rust, you have ferrous metal.

Most ferrous metals also have magnetic properties. My husband carries a little magnet that a scrap yard handed out as a promotional gift and he uses it whenever he has any questions regarding the type of metal when he is sorting metal.

Non-ferrous metals include aluminum, brass, copper, nickel, tin, lead, and zinc. Gold and silver are also non- ferrous metals.

They are non-magnetic.

For the most part, ferrous scrap metals tend to be in good supply, so the prices tend to be lower than most non-ferrous metals.

Because steel and iron alloys are constantly being recycled in high volume all over the globe, the prices for these materials stay fairly constant on a month-to-month basis, dropping or raising only slightly.

Non-ferrous scrap, as we mentioned before, are somewhat harder to come by and more difficult to create. This makes the demand higher, which drives up the price per pound higher than ferrous metals.

While aluminum prices don't fluctuate often, other metal like copper and brass can change drastically in just a month's time depending on the needs of the market. Interesting fact - Aluminum is currently the third most recycled material in the world.

A Quick Overview on Different Types of Metal

Below is a brief overview of various metal types. I found this website

http://iscrapapp.com/metals/

I really like it as it shows color photos of the various metal types too so you may want to use it for a more detailed reference. Below is our quick overview to give you something to think with regarding metal types.

Copper

You may have heard stories of copper theft or copper wire theft. This is because copper is a very high payout metal and unfortunately we have to deal with thieves stealing it – which makes scrappers look bad. As I said earlier, someone stealing scrap is not a scrapper, they are a thief.

Copper is often the metal of choice for older plumbing. Copper is also in wires – as in the plug in cord for a vacuum or stereo. I cannot tell you how many times I have been junking only to find a scrapper cut the cord off a perfectly nice stereo.

I don't go along with the idea of stopping at a home and cutting the electric cord off a curbside find. Many do it though so you will need to decide if you feel it is okay to do or not. Then you need to take the cord home and remove the copper wire. It will take a lot of cords, and time to remove the copper wire, to add up to anything substantial weight wise.

Cast Iron #1 Iron

Cast Iron can be a real money maker for you. This is the very heavy metal you may recall seeing in older bath tubs and sinks. It is very heavy so be careful when lifting it, you may need a helper to get it in your vehicle.

My experience is as an average street scrapper, unless you live in an area where someone is renovating older homes, you will not come across many bath tubs but you may occasionally come across a sink once in a great while.

Heavy Steel #2 Iron

You will usually find this type of metal in oil tanks as an example.

My experience is that as an average street scrapper, you will not come across this metal.

Stainless Steel

This may be a type of metal that you find a decent amount of. Kitchen sinks are a good example. Some posts and pans may fall in this category also.

There are some sinks with more nickel. If a magnet hardly sticks to the sink it probably has more nickel. You can sort the two – more nickel and less nickel and see if the scrap yard you use pays differently for each. If not, then definitely don't waste your time sorting in the future.

Light Iron

This will probably be what you find the most of when you scrap. This is any steel that isn't one of the type above. Stoves, washers, dryers, freezers, shelves, shoe racks, bikes and much more. The list is long but I think this gives you an idea.

Aluminum

This light weight metal is often found on summer folding chairs – you probably know the ones that I am referring to. You will need to remove the webbing material before you take them to the scrap yard. Some gutters and siding is aluminum but look carefully as more and more is vinyl. Some baking pans and sheets are aluminum also. Occasionally you will find pieces of aluminum on the curb, maybe from various household projects.

Lead

Lead is often the metal used in those heavy old plumbing pipes in older homes as well as water and drain pipes in older homes. Lead pipes are deceptively heavy. You'll notice when you pick one up that it feels unusually heavy compared to other pipes.

You will also find lead in car, boat and lawnmower batteries. Shop your batteries around as there can be quite a price jump between scrap yards. I've seen between $3-$8 pricewise. The nice thing is, many garbage companies will not take them so they sit on the curb. However scrappers know the value and snap them up. I have seen hand written signs offering to pay $2-$3 for batteries. Those people are, I am guessing, then hauling them to the scrap yard that pays more and making a profit.

Yellow Brass

A magnet will not stick to brass. I listed it as yellow brass as I see it commonly called that but you may see it just listed as brass.

Older faucets are often made of brass. Sometimes you will get brass from older plumbing pipes too.

Other Metal Opportunities

This section may apply more to a seasoned scrapper but I want to at least give you some insight.

Some items contain a mix of metals.

A car radiator is a great example. A radiator is usually aluminum with copper or brass tubing running through it.

Check with your local scrapyards as many will accept radiators. Be sure to price shop their payouts if you have more than one scrap yard in the area.

Electric motors are another mixed metal opportunity. So- motors in vacuums, fans, etc. may be worth pulling and selling separately as they usually have a mix of copper and/or aluminum inside. They often have a copper coating and often have a good amount of plastic too.

Some scrap yards will have a separate area for electric motors and radiators. Call and query or ask for a list when you visit the scrap yards.

Some scrap yards post prices before you enter and others do not.

It pays, often tremendously, to shop the prices before you go to a scrap yard.

Just because one paid a certain amount a month, or even week ago, does not mean they pay the same today. This used to drive me crazy but now I've gotten used to it. The prices will fluctuate. What is the worst feeling though is when you haul a load in and go back the same day in the afternoon and see the price dropped and you are down twenty, thirty or even more dollars less than the load in the morning. Most post in the morning but I have seen rates changed midday.

Once you are moving along with scrapping, you may find that you work with two, three or even more scrap yards depending upon the various metals that you accumulate.

Typical Scrap

Each scrap yard is different so I would ask for a list of what they accept, plus you want to compare prices against other scrap yards.

Below is a list of what one scrap yard accepts

Aluminum Cans

Appliances

Copper

Aluminum Siding

Brass

Scrap Steel

Wire

Electric Motors

Stainless Steel

Radiators

PVC Siding

PVC Tubing & Fencing

Plastic

Paper

Cardboard

Batteries

Tire rims

Things You Commonly Cannot Scrap

Check with the individual yard but this is a common list.

City, County or State owned material

Empty or full whole compressed gas cylinders (e.g. oxygen, acetylene, Propane and Freon tanks.)

Computer monitors or televisions

Fluorescent light fixtures that have PCB containing ballasts. A ballast specifying that it does not contain PCB's is acceptable.

Tires

Sealed drums

Rail Road scrap

Utility Owned Scrap

Beer Kegs

Items Containing Radiation, Asbestos or Lead Paint

Nickel-Cadmium or Radioactive materials

Capacitors, transformers with PCB's

Bulk phone books

Items containing Freon – sometimes they will have someone there to remove Freon or deduct cost from your payout.

Your Clients

There are many, many good people who will flag you down in a subdivision and say they have metal. The metal may be one tiny bar or several appliances. Either way, you should always thank them and be courteous.

These people are your clients.

You can print up business cards on your computer or order them online for often less than ten dollars.

If you decide scrapping is for you, you may want to invest in business cards.

People may ask for your number or may ask if you have a card.

We also bought magnetic signs for the trucks advertising appliance and swimming pool haul away.

Your goal is to constantly be building a good group of clients.

Clients will watch for you. They will refer people to you. They will also be positive and stick up for you if there is a whiner on the block – remember the two metal chairs I mentioned earlier?

People You Want to Avoid

As mentioned earlier, there are also some nasty people on the planet.

Not just people who live in subdivisions where you are scrapping but also fellow scrappers. Use caution and use common sense.

I've seen people run to the curb and pull out junk so a scrapper wouldn't take it. This was junk that was placed on the curb for pickup.

I've seen people heckle scrappers.

I've seen people come running out to the street screeching at a scrapper to slow down, when the driver was going well below the speed limit.

We've also turned down the "opportunity" for my husband to go in to more than one home with people who just seemed to be up to something.

We will discuss handling difficult people later in this book but I will say now, if you have a short temper – seriously, scrapping isn't for you.

You also need to keep your guard up.

You may think I'm wasting time telling you about good and bad experiences but I want to ensure you are prepared for both good and bad people.

Otherwise, a bad person may ruin your day or cause problems for you with the police. You also may find yourself in a dangerous situation. You need to be ready and understand how to handle a problem person.

You also need to know how to recognize quality clients as they will often result in repeat business or referrals.

Be courteous to everyone and focus on growing a good base of repeat business and referrals.

Dumpsters, Businesses and Construction Sites

Dumpsters are on private property such as businesses and new home construction. I highly advise NOT touching those dumpsters.

You may be considered a trespasser if so.

Plus, if it is a new home build, the contractor probably has equipment and materials nearby – someone could report seeing your vehicle and if something is missing from that work site – hello police visit.

Many contractors have existing arrangements with others to remove the scrap or they themselves remove the scrap.

If you want to approach a job site and see if they will let you take the scrap – that is your choice.

We did so once and the guy said he would sell us the material for a hundred dollars or something along that line. We declined.

I do know of one scrapper who does had relationships with various construction sites to take the scrap but it may take you some time to establish the relationships.

As far as businesses, we approached a business about their scrap and the business owner agreed to let us take the materials. The agreement as that my husband would move the materials outside – against the building and then remove at close of business.

We went back and took a few pieces as the metal was larger. We returned less than thirty minutes later and thieves had taken the rest of our load.

Your Appearance

You always should be neatly dressed.

Your shirt and pants may get dirty fast. Keep a spare shirt in your vehicle.

Make sure you wear sturdy shoes or boots.

I suggest purchasing a lightweight rain coat with a hood.

Don't look like you just rolled out of bed or our of a bramble bush.

Speak clearly and nicely and don't forget the please and thank you.

Your vehicle should be clean inside and outside.

If a possible client comes up to your vehicle window, he shouldn't look inside and see a filthy vehicle or an unkempt person.

I'll also be blunt here – people are less inclined to call the police about a "suspicious person" if you are neatly dressed.

If you are stopped by the police, I think you will fare better if you are neatly dressed and organized versus someone who looks like they haven't washed in days.

Setting Up

There are a few things you need to have beforehand and need to research

Each city and town has different policies and ordinances regarding scrapping.

You are solely responsible for finding out if scrapping is allowed, if there are certain times it is allowed, if there are registration fees etc.

You need to have a place to store your scrap at home. If you have neighbors who are a pain – you may need to install a fence. We had to and so did one fellow scrapper. In both cases, I think the problem neighbors sprang from pure jealousy but will talk about problem neighbors later in this book.

You need to have a reliable and safe vehicle to collect and transport the items that you collect. Ideally, if you have two vehicles, all the better. We will talk more about vehicles later in this book.

You need to know the locations and hours of local scrap yards.

As you progress you'll learn who pays the most for each type of material.

Some yards will pay or newspapers, vinyl siding and other materials.

You should have bins or garbage cans for sorting your materials.

You should have the following:

Safety glasses/goggles

Sturdy gloves

Bins for sorting

Tools – see the separate chapter which follows on tools please.

Rope for tying things in your vehicle

Red flags to tie on the back of your vehicle if any items are hanging out

If you have a truck, I highly suggest building sides on the bed. Most people use wood but I have also seen metal racks.

You do not want the height of the racks to be too high. I personally like them with slats but you can use solid pieces of wood too. The main thing is – make it look neat. We have painted racks black to match a black truck and we have left them as natural wood.

You do not want any loose wood hanging off.

You can add a small trailer but let's wait until you get your feet wet first.

Pen and notebook.

Your business cards- this can wait until you're a bit established but definitely keep the pen and notebook in your vehicle.

Tools

This area is my husband's specialty, so I have watched him take apart metal to give you an idea of the must have tools and equipment that will be of help to you.

Some of these items you may luck out and find while scrapping. Others you will need to procure.

Goggles/safety glasses – this is a MUST HAVE.

Study gloves – another MUST HAVE. We go through packs of gloves so if you can buy in bulk, do so. You will use them when scrapping, when unloading and when you are disassembling metal.

Hammer – my husband has a selection but he has also accumulated many curbside finds. You will use your hammer's claw to pry things open or loose. Plus if you are taking something apart, you may need to be hitting it with a sturdy hammer.

Sledge Hammer – this will help you smash plastic off of items and when breaking up metal objects.

Drills – my husband uses a couple different electric cordless drills. He has Phillips and a flat head screwdriver bits. You may find curbside drills too as you spend time scrapping.

Screwdrivers – he has an assortment of screwdrivers.

Metal snips – one is always in the truck and he has a few on hand in the garage.

Reciprocating Saw – we buy metal cutting blades and he uses this saw often. We have bought the best of the line and the cheaper knockoffs. You will go through these saws – do not try to take back to your hardware store and get a new one after you've worn this one out – and if you are a serious scrapper – you will go through these. This is a tool of the trade. Don't make a bad name for yourself at the local hardware store by trying to return tools you've worn out. I know in this area, at least two scrappers have told me that a certain big box home improvement store will not accept returns from them. Unfortunately, these two men abused the return policy and now they are labeled by the store. Not something that you ever want to occur.

Plastic totes – curbside finds and great for sorting. You can also use buckets – again curbside finds. We have not bought totes or buckets since we started scrapping as they are usually abundant curbside finds. Sometimes you will find a pail curbside with used tools inside which is a nice extra bonus.

Magnet – as mentioned before, my husband has a little magnet that a scrap yard gave him. It is on a little pencil type stick with a magnet on the end. He keeps one in the truck and a few in the garage.

Organizing Your Metal

This is often a several hour project. Make sure you have your safety glasses on and wear sturdy gloves.

Get your bins lined up and start methodically working through your metal. If possible, it may go faster if you do batches – all your grills in a batch for example. You will get your own routine soon enough.

As my husband takes aluminum to a separate yard, he will often set aluminum aside and work on what is going to one specific yard. I can tell where we are going that day by what metal he is working on.

Large empty garbage cans are also handy for organizing – again, these are often curbside finds. If the bottom is broken, duct tape works wonders.

The main way my husband disassembles is by using his drill. He has a couple cordless drills charging at all times so he can keep moving.

If you want to have a detailed primer on dissembling something such as a stove for example, you can check YouTube. Just search for scrapping a stove for example. But, in our case – appliances such as stoves, go straight to the scrap yard, they are not disassembled.

I know some scrappers do take things like appliances apart and sort the metals. We do not do so.

If you have plumbing pipes, the reciprocal saw may come in handy to take apart copper and other metals. For example, often the joint where copper and brass meet is one you want to saw apart. Do not forget those safety goggles!

Remember though, there is scrap waiting while you are organizing so determine what tasks bring you the most revenue.

For example – I would not advise disassembling a stove and taking 30 minutes to do so.

You are wasting time that could be spent picking up a truck full of scrap.

The one thing my husband has ingrained in my head is this – the one minute we spend picking up a tiny piece of metal or wasting time getting out the door to scrap is the one minute that could make or break getting a full pile of metal or a stove or whatever.

I will repeat this later when we wrap up and you will see this happen many times. Hopefully in your favor, but sometimes not.

Determining Your Best Profit Routes

You will be using the notebook to keep track of gas per day and miles per day. These are both tax deductions at the end of the year if you declare your earnings from scrap. You also need to keep all receipts. Talk with your accountant about tax deductions and mileage.

But, either way, the information is also going to help you determine the best days for the maximum return on your time and gas money.

For example –

We know 5 towns/cities in the area have garbage pickup Monday, Tuesday, Wednesday, Thursday and Friday.

So on Monday we fill our gas tank for a cost of $40 dollars.

We note this cost in our notebook.

We drive to Town 1.

We establish a route, driving methodically from one end of town to the other.

We observe there are at least 6 other scrap trucks when we go at 5PM. 3 of those trucks are almost full.

We drive for 3 hours plus 15 minutes each way to get to the town from our town. So we have 4 hours of time invested.

We determine how much gas has been used. We note how many miles we drove and the time spent.

We deduct the gas price from the price we are paid at the scrap yard.

Next week, we go to the same town 30 minutes earlier. Why? Remember those 3 trucks that were almost full? Were they full because they had scrapped elsewhere or because they started earlier or because all 3 had a banner day?

We should be able, by process of elimination, to determine which of the above three reasons fits the "why" regarding the 3 trucks being full.

You will usually see the same scrappers each week. You will often see fellow scrappers in other towns/cities. There may be some who are downright rude or even flip you off but most are cordial and like you, are just out looking for a way to earn additional money. We will talk more about being cordial and interacting with other scrappers later in this book.

After a few weeks' time of keeping notes you may find that one town is better than another or that if three towns have the same pickup day, which one to go to first and which one you may want to pass on.

The main thing is you MUST keep statistics if you want to run this as a business and want to be profitable.

There will be various factors to consider. Factors include:

Time of year

Time of day

Weather

Sports – if football is on TV that day for example

Kid's sports – for example if many subdivisions have plenty of children, those children (and their parents) may be at baseball or football practice. One of those practice days may fall the night before garbage day so scrap may be put out earlier, before they go to practice, or later than usual, when they return from practice.

Demographics of subdivisions in city/town – for example, many upper income working class versus older retired upper income

You will probably find additional factors once you have established a routine such as:

Number of fellow scrappers

Average amount of scrap on curb – some towns/cities and subdivisions in those town/cities may be plentiful as far as scrap potential and some scarce.

Then you may have unusual factors unique to your area such as:

I won't divulge the city in this book but I know of at least one city in which city employees, on the clock, drive around supposedly looking for branches to collect and pick up scrap instead.

I know of a town where certain people scrap yet police pull over others and inform them that there is a "no scrapping" ordinance.

Choose your battles wisely. It just isn't worth going up against matters like the two I just mentioned. Move on to another area instead or change your route.

Timing

You will need to establish a routine and this may be based upon your open schedule too.

For example, you may get up at 5:30 in the morning to scrap.

But keep in mind, how many people put out garbage at 5:30? If most people put out garbage the night before, any scrap or junk is most likely picked up that night.

If you are in a community with a lot of commuters, 5:30 may be a perfect time. In another neighborhood, 7:00 in the morning may be better.

I've seen plentiful scrap picked up at 3:30 in the afternoon some weeks and other weeks nothing until 7:30pm.

You need to get used to the routine in each town/city and then also each subdivision in that town/city and plan your routine accordingly.

Don't forget to factor in things that may change a schedule for a day or a season as we just discussed earlier.

Placement of Items

This is a tricky topic as unfortunately there are occasional people who are troublemakers or who I think want to turn in a claim to their insurance.

There are also kids who want new bikes.

Then we have people who place scrap or junk on the curb and suddenly when a scrapper pulls up the item is priceless.

They come running out and yank the item from the curb. I've seen males and females do this and to be honest, I really do not want an item coming from the home of someone so petty so it rolls right off me and doesn't bother me. This person has way more issues than a scrapper. Just keep driving.

Usually.........an item, such as a washer, is placed on the curb next to the garbage.

Sometimes, people will place items out before they bring out their garbage. It depends on the community. In some cities/towns, there are ordinances regarding what time garbage may be placed on the curb so you may not see much garbage on the curb until after a certain time.

You may notice that many subdivisions appear to have residents who all come home around a certain time. Then you may need to do two passes through that subdivision. The first one covers those who bring things to the curb right when they come home and the second pass covers those who wait until later in the evening. In some cases, there may even be a third round to cover those who wait until right before bedtime.

You'll learn the routine for each area.

But the most important thing is determining if something is out for trash pickup or left – accidently or not- on the curb.

When in doubt – ask or pass. By asking, you do not ask a child, you ask the homeowner.

Usually I would say just pass but there may be an occasion where it is too good to pass but still questionable.

You need to be careful as often people mow their lawn the night before garbage pickup.

So just because a mower and weed whacker are on the curb does not mean they are being thrown out. In most cases they are not – most cases being 99.9 percent of the time.

Even if the garbage is on the curb, the mower and weed whacker may have been left out while someone ran in the house to eat or whatever.

Bikes are a whole discussion on their own. Children often have a bad habit of tossing down a bike- on the curb. If a bike is being thrown out it is usually right by the garbage can but.........we have the children factor to consider.

I know of one situation where a scrapper saw a bike in among the garbage cans. He asked a boy who was about 12 years of age if the bike was scrap and was told yes.

A few minutes later as he was driving, he was flagged down by a woman in a car who told him he took her son's bike. He gave her the bike back but explained – he had asked the child beforehand. Fortunately, she believed him and was highly irritated at her son.

On the other hand, the same scrapper saw a high end bike in among the garbage cans, knocked on the door and the gentleman said yes, the bike was in the garbage as his son had outgrown it. It was a $600 bike. These finds are not common but do occur.

There are other cool finds that I hope you also come across.

My husband and I have a beautiful mantle clock, appraised at over $500. It was placed on top of a garbage can for pick up. It was missing a key. I called the manufacturer and paid $20 for a new key.

In our area, people will often place nice items on top of a closed garbage can. I've also seen little card tables set up with a sign that states the items are free.

Under no circumstances should you open garbage cans or garbage bags.

If there are boxes next to the garbage cans, you can determine if they are full or empty after a bit of practice. People will often toss garbage in a new box so proceed with caution. You do not want to make a mess.

On the flip side, I have several new small appliances, including a name brand food processor, still brand new, wrapped in plastic, in the box.

On the icky side – and I'm sorry but I feel I need to give you the icky side too – there are people who are just nasty. My husband stopped to pick up a like new electric car for kids. You know the type. They are plentiful in this area but this one was extra nice. For whatever reason, whoever put it out filled the seat and floor with dog potty. Disgusting, yes. Why? Who knows? Just keep moving.

Unfortunately, due to the economy, there are more and more homes being vacated. The end of the month and the first of the month are typical times and occasionally the 15th of the month.

If garbage pickup day falls on the first or end of the month, you may turn the corner in a subdivision and see a pile beyond belief.

If the garbage pickup day falls a day or two after, the pile is usually well picked over by others, often on the block, by the time you find it.

If you are coming across massive piles, please do not start ripping open boxes like a kid on Christmas day. You may need to accept the fact that you need to take an entire box, often labeled, home and then you can go through it at home and pitch what you don't want.

We ended up taking numerous boxes home. Contents included a high end nativity, expensive Christmas decorations, expensive toys, an enormous amount of empty DVD cases, used hair and bath products, a ton of plastic hangers and a few name brand clothes. So we ended up with about 4 large bag of trash when we were done but the great finds outweighed the garbage.

I will tell you now, curbside treasures usually do not last long. Even non scrappers will join in if they drive by and see a nice lamp or headboard especially in the nicer neighborhoods.

My husband is beyond a good person and has numerous times, collected beautiful furniture, including a little girl's bedroom set which he then delivered to needy families.

He simply couldn't bear the thought of like new furniture going to a garbage dump when there are so many needy people.

It only takes a call or two to a local shelter to find out if they need furniture or know of families who may.

I am not sure why people do not run an ad for free furniture or do not donate to a local Goodwill store but for whatever reason, at least in this area, very nice stuff is often tossed on the curb. This is not just vacated homes.

While often it is a no brainer to determine something is on the curb for pickup, still use care. Most common items NOT out for pickup, even though they may be on the curb

Lawn mowers

Lawn equipment

Basketball hoop – portable

Bikes

Fire pits

Another interesting occurrence is placement of usually a large metal object such as a washer, dryer or in one case, a very large dog cage – placed right next to garbage containers. On these items is a very small, handwritten, often note size, often flipped over – note that reads "For Sale".

While more times than not, people will write Free on a piece of paper or FREE, works fine or Free needs (and they list what is wrong, such as needs belt, needs whatever), we have the occasional oddball who does the opposite.

In this case, we have people placing an item, on the curb or street, mixed in alongside garbage cans. I'm sorry but unless this person is quite elderly, I cannot fathom why anyone would do this unless they are trying to cause a problem.

I assure you that if you stop and knock on the door to clarify, item is on curb, you will be told it is for sale and not in the trash.

In speaking with a couple police officers, they do receive calls from people that their mower was "stolen". I'm sorry but I definitely don't think that was the case. I think people either intentionally put it on the curb with the micro sign, put it on the curb hoping it is taken or are one of the many I see each week who are cutting the lawn and leave the mower on the curb. I just don't get it at all.

Then we have the person who tries to sell you their scrap. This comes down usually one of two ways;

You are flagged down, asked if you collect metal. In many cases the flagger has watched you picking up metal at his neighbor's and/or sees that you have a vehicle full of scrap.

Then the person says oh, I have a, in this case we will say a stove, in my house. Then they say, well how much do you get for it at the scrap yard? Once you say a number, they try to sell you the item for usually around 5 dollars less than you just said.

Then we have the other one who cuts to the chase and says, hey I have a stove, I want 30 bucks for it – do you want it.

These people just simply have no clue regarding what goes in to scrapping. They may have seen an ad from a scrap company regarding paying cash for scrap and seem to think you are going to make a few hundred dollars for a small amount of metal.

My personal advice is- do not pay cash for someone's garbage. I recently saw a nice Volvo with the back seat removed and a washer crammed in. This person lived at least 30 minutes from a scrap yard. Scrap yards are hectic and busy. You unload your items yourself. You then need to show ID and fill out paperwork. So the 10 bucks he will make before gas costs will cost him about an hour and a half of his time minimum.

I also have seen people offer a large amount of scrap and then as the final piece is loaded in, ask well how much will you be getting for all of this? As though you are hauling away gold bricks. The best way to handle this sort is to nicely say, well before my gas money, I get around ten cents a pound. This seems to put things in perspective for this type of person.

Then we also have the ones who have an item on the curb, in the case of this story, it was a rusted out grill.

The homeowner was standing nearby talking with another man. The scrapper asked if the grill was scrap. The man looked at his neighbor friend and said, oh I don't know. "Do you want it?" to his friend. The friend said yes. Now we all know there was no interest in the grill until the scrapper asked about it. That grill sat in the friend's truck bed for over two months.

I don't try to figure out why some people feel the need to act that way and I advise you to be the same way – don't let idiots ruin your day.

The scrapper marked that house off his list based on the above experience.

Cycles

You will soon see that there are different cycles for different things – for example:

Grills – curbside placement increases end of summer, early summer and right around Father's Day

Lawn mowers – follows a similar pattern as grills

Snow blowers – early winter. I think due to people deciding to buy a new one or better one. Occasionally one in the summer if someone cleans their garage.

Lawn spreaders – spring and late fall. These are mainly plastic but nice if you need one for personal use or resale

Hose reels – spring and late fall. Again mainly all plastic but nice if you need one.

Patio sets – spring and fall

Patio cushions – often like new – mainly in the fall

Planters – usually in the fall

Decorative patio heaters – usually in the fall

Sofas – spring and whenever local stores have big promotions. Sometimes also right before Christmas holidays. You need to use care with sofas and living room chairs. More on this later in this book.

Beds – whenever local stores have big promotions

TVs – Black Friday and throughout the summer

Appliances – these will surface on the curb based on local sales in your area

Christmas decorations – before and after Christmas

Suitcases – many like new. They are not metal but nice if you need one or a few. These are usually available year around and most often at the end of summer and after Black Friday

Dishes – usually after Black Friday and before Christmas. I have seen complete sets, often like new in the box.

Coffee pots – not a week goes by when I do not see one on the curb

Blenders – usually after Black Friday and before Christmas. Most often like new.

Food processors – often new in the box. Usually fall through winter but sometimes year around.

Are you getting excited? I am often speechless over our curbside finds. I do think people truly want to find a good home for these items as things like suitcases, dishes etc. are often neatly packed and sitting in a prominent place on the curb.

Remember, people usually move the beginning or the end of the month.

Moving piles are either very neatly organized or a crazy mess on the curb. Do your best not to make a mess when you pick through the items. If the pile seems too messy, unless you see a real find, just keep driving. The neighbor may not recall the pile was a disaster before you arrived but they may instead blame you for making a mess.

People usually do at least one good spring or fall garage cleaning – or both

The week before Thanksgiving people tend to clean.

Garage sales often result in items placed on the curb before or after.

You may notice different patterns on your routes but you will start to see patterns if you pay attention.

Advertising

While I think most of your business will come from driving your routes and possibly repeat clients, you may want to consider advertising.

I do not suggest paid advertising in the beginning.

You may want to create a simple flyer and post copies in places such as local grocery stores, gas stations and senior citizens.

Haul away services is a good title but you do need to be specific. What will you haul away?

Some people will clean out a basement, garage or a whole house often with the understanding that they keep everything. The problem is you may end up with a lot of unusable things that you need to dispose of.

Scrap yards will not take TVS, computers and other items. These items are the ones that you may end up with when doing a clean out so you need to determine if this type of project is worth your time.

The nice thing about picking up some haul away jobs is that most are done on the weekend so you are not missing out on scrapping.

While we have had some decent haul away jobs – this is an example of a good deal gone bad.

The guy was referred by someone to us. He was remodeling his home and had metal. He said there was some wood and concrete that would be part of the haul away. He also stated that he buys and flips homes and there would be more projects. So we went to the site.

His garage was filled – a two car garage – filled with debris. He insisted that we take all the debris first and then the metal last.

My husband loaded wood from the garage for a long while.

The guy told us there was a dump "just a short ways away". The dump he was referring to closed years ago as we soon found out after driving around for well over thirty minutes. We had to go to another dump way out of our way.

My husband had wanted to go back the next day to finish as it was very hot and the dump excursion had taken us way off course time wise as we had a scrap route in the afternoon.

The guy, who was pleasant enough overall, was a bit fussy and wanted us to finish that day. He was fussy that it took so long to come back and we explained – the dump he mentioned was closed long ago. So we loaded the second truck of debris and the guy announced he had to go to work.

Now being blunt, he could have let us come back and take the metal but he wanted us to come back the next day in the morning. My husband said we could come midday, not morning.

We took the debris that afternoon and dumped it.

We went back the next day and the guy wasn't there.

The drive was out of our way but near a scrap yard we went to so my husband said, okay, we will come back the next day when we delivered scrap.

Long story short – several days past and we went to the home and also called – with no luck.

Finally after almost a week, we connected with the guy and he said oh – we hadn't come back.........so he gave the metal to someone else.

My husband said, yes we had.....

Turns out the person who referred us – conveniently took the metal. Yes you read that right. I think we were set up by both of them. The client did give my husband twenty dollars – to cover his gas.......

Needless to say we never heard from the supposed house flipper again and we will never take another referral from this person again.

That was a very bitter pill to swallow but I hope our experience gives you some insight so you never make the same mistake.

If you establish yourself in the area or with senior citizen groups you may establish a good client base with repeat business and referrals.

I have tried Yellow Page ads – total waste of money and it was not cheap.

I have thought about the restaurant placemat ads but when you look at your average weekly scrap income – you need to determine if investing in paid advertising will result in a profit.

I am all for testing and measuring marketing sources but I would test and measure free ones first – posting ads in grocery stores, senior centers and other places where you may attract a new client or two.

I do think if you look professional, are polite and friendly that you will see your business grow without paid advertising.

Sorting scrap metal

You have a couple choices before you sell your scrap.

You can sort the metal by metal type and sell each type individually.

Sometimes you can do this at one scrap yard other times it may pay off to sell one type of metal, for example, aluminum at one scrap yard and another type of metal, for example copper, elsewhere.

I suggest picking up a few curbside find plastic totes and use them to hold your sorted metal.

Depending on the scrap yard, you may be charged or have money deducted from your scrap for things such as plastic, wood, Freon (such as inside a freezer or refrigerator), chair webbing, etc.

Some scrap yards may have a percentage limit on plastic.

I've seen some people just haul in a load and scrap in the general scrap pile.

I've watched items that have a mix of metal just tossed in the general heap.

The scrapper makes less money than if he/she would have sorted the metal but perhaps the person doesn't have room at home, or time or isn't able to take the metal apart.

In most cases it is best to be able to sort and separate the metal, dispose of plastic and then go to a couple different scrap yards but if you are already working a 40 hour week and have limited space, using the general drop off may be best for you.

You will develop your own routine.

Neighbors and Your Scrap

Do not leave a truck full of scrap on the street overnight or unattended during the day if you are in a high theft area.

We live in an average middle to upper income city. We have had bikes and other metal removed from our trucks several times. While I do not think it was any of our neighbors, I think someone driving by at night felt it was too easy to pass up and helped themselves.

I definitely would never leave a truck with scrap unattended in a shopping center parking lot.

Regarding neighbors, if you have some close by, I'm sure you try to be a "good neighbor" but unfortunately, you may have someone on your block or even next door who, for whatever reason, has an issue with you scrapping.

Before you begin scrapping, I suggest that if you are not taking scrap straight to the scrap yard daily that you ensure you have a secure location, perhaps in your garage, to unload and sort.

If you are sorting, it may take you several days or weeks to get enough of one type of metal. So having the plastic totes we discussed earlier helps tremendously.

If you are scrapping on a regular basis, you may find that you are leaving your home right at dawn or in the winter, when it is still dark.

Ideally, if you are unloading metal, do so the night before so you are not clunking around too early in the morning. I highly doubt that you will be making so much noise unloading as to disturb someone but again, we want to always be a good neighbor.

I have heard this story from at least one other scrapper and I will tell you the same – if you start scrapping, prepare to erect a fence if needed.

In our case, we had repeated problems with a renter in a home next door. First came the calls to the police department regarding "junk" on our drive.

This resulted in a couple visits from the police department. They were very nice, saw we had an organized line of mowers that my husband was preparing to deliver to our wholesale buyer.

The officer stated that he saw no issue with our drive and the call was unfounded.

I asked him if erecting a fence would be wise and was told that yes, if possible. Even though we were not told to clean up anything – there was nothing to clean up. But the fine folks next door couldn't see the drive if we had a fence.

Plus we had several challenges with children next door running onto our driveway. Keep in mind when you are backing up a truck full of metal, you do not need the fear of a child darting onto your property and in your path.

These people had issues beyond scrap as once they saw that their calls didn't work, they then began making frivolous calls stating we were parked on our lawn which is against city ordinance.

The local police were more than pleasant to us and after a couple calls of that nature, the police just would drive by our home, see we were indeed not on the lawn and then keep driving.

In one case, the officer stopped, said our truck tire was slightly grazing our lawn and the fact that these people called about this really enlightened the police department on the caliber of our neighbors.

If you do have a visit from a police officer, I trust that you will be respectful and nice. Understand their position – they have to respond to complaints even when they arrive and see there is no real cause. Personally I wish police would start fining those who make frivolous complaints.

So, after having enough of the constant problems due to the frivolous calls, we staked off our property to erect a fence.

That day, the landlord of the home next door came storming over and was carrying on that we could not erect a fence.

He was yelling at me that he was calling the police. Well, I'm sure he did and by now, they had quite a reputation with the police for making frivolous calls. Now they were making a ludicrous one – regarding our erecting a fence on our own property. The police must have explained that if we are erecting a fence on our property, well.....what is the problem?

You may be wondering why these people carried on the way that they did.

There are some people who delight in being spiteful.

Please keep in mind, that before we erected a fence we spoke with our family attorney and also the city to ensure we followed ordinances and had permits if needed – none were needed in our case.

After the fence was erected the problems did not cease, the neighbors were tossing nails, screws and glass along with countless cigarette butts over the fence.

Once they moved (finally) the debris stopped appearing on the drive – 100 percent stopped.

I cannot tell you how many flat tires we had during that time. I was walking the drive several times a day and filled baggies with debris which I kept to show police in case they were called again by these people.

A fellow scrapper had challenges similar to ours and erected a 7 foot fence which is the tallest you can erect. Our fence is 6 foot.

So the neighbor called the police because his fence was 7 foot tall. Go figure. Needless to say, the police came out, measured, said it met the ordinance and left.

I do hope you will have good neighbors. All our other neighbors are good. They give us scrap and junk. They stop by if they see an appliance on the curb down the street.

We also help out neighbors who need a mower or basketball hoop. We don't take money from them for these items – that is a personal choice.

However, you do need to be cautious as my husband gave a couple bikes to someone two streets over and then found out the guy scrapped them for money. So, no more freebies for him. Scrapping is hard work. It takes time and gas money and while you want to be a good neighbor and don't mind helping a neighbor, you shouldn't feel bad about standing firm against someone trying to scam you.

Getting Paid for Scrap

Each yard is different but the basic overall plan is usually as follows:

You will most likely be required to provide a state ID or driver's license.

In some cases you are assigned a sticker or paper with your account number. This stays in your vehicle.

Depending on the type of scrap, you may drive over a large scale.

If so your vehicle weight is noted. You unload the metal and then drive back over the scale. The vehicle weight is then noted again.

In smaller yards, you may pull up, place your various types of metal into containers and then the containers are weighed.

Saturdays tend to be busiest.

Most yards close early on Saturday and are closed Sunday and holidays.

Most scrap yards open around 7 or 8 and close around 4 during the week.

The weight per ton may change.

Previously we would see the price per ton go up in cold weather to motivate people to come in but this past year we have noticed the price drop in cold weather months at least one yard.

Loading Scrap versus Junk in Your Vehicle

You may pick up both scrap and junk or you may pick up just one of the two.

With scrap, you can cram it in your vehicle as it doesn't matter if something is broke, bent or scuffed.

With junking, you are going to clean and repair as needed and then sell the item so care is needed.

You may pick up a mix of the two.

If that is the case, you need to determine how to place the stuff in your vehicle.

You will soon realize that some items are way more solid than you realize and others are not.

If you are picking up a mix of scrap and junk, keep a couple heavy towels and/or a blanket in your vehicle to pad fragile items.

What to Do With Items Too Good to Scrap

You may start accumulating some interesting stuff and realize it is really too nice to scrap.

If you are handy, you can repair washers and dryers, clean and resell. I know of a fairly well to do neighbor who does exactly this.

If you are handy you can repair TVs and lawn mowers and just about anything else depending upon your repair ability.

Not good at repairing mowers? Is there someone in town selling used mowers? It may be worth asking him if he would be interested in buying used mowers from you.

You also may want to visit your local flea market and see if anyone sells mowers.

I'm not talking about someone selling an occasional mower, although you could ask them. I am referring to someone who sells mowers weekly, he usually will have several.

Remember, when reselling, the other person needs to make money too. If you can establish a regular buyer, it may be a good thing to be able to sell 5 to 10 non- working mowers each week for $5 to $15 or more depending upon your area.

You may decide to keep the items for your own personal use. Being able to save paying $75 for a like new kid's bike isn't a bad deal.

Want to decorate your lawn for Christmas? Why pay $100 for a snowman when you can pick him up on the curb? Yes you may have to pick it up after Christmas and store in your garage until next winter but...you just saved $$$.

Christmas lights – same thing. Abundant usually right around Thanksgiving when people buy new sets and pitch the old ones. Same with Christmas trees. I've seen tubs of ornaments, still in packaging, on the curb.

Kid's toys are often abundant curbside finds. Skateboards and scooters – often well- loved but still workable are usually easy finds.

Need plastic totes? I refuse to pay $12 or more for one when they are often abundant on the curb.

Traveling? Curbside suitcases are often like new.

Kid size plastic picnic table needed for outdoor parties? It is highly possible to find one curbside.

Have a child going to college? With a little planning you can furnish his/her apartment with nice lamps and used furniture.

This is where I wanted to remember to discuss sofas and living room furniture with you. This is a tip that I received from a lady who ran a local resale shop. I would call her when I saw nice large curbside finds that we had no use for or had no room in the truck. She and her daughter ran a nice resale shop in town and often ran the same scrap route looking for items to sell. She advised me to be very careful with sofas as sometimes they may have pet urine or fleas. With that being said, pay attention before picking up a sofa or living room chair.

Some resale shops will buy used items.

Other shops will arrange a consignment payout with you.

You can also hold a garage sale.

My husband and I were going to visit a friend and drove by a home with a beautiful mirror on the curb. My husband saw the look on my face and said on our way home we would pick it up. I said to him that it would be long gone by then. He agreed and turned around. We had not even gone a block when we went back.

It was gone. Yes, that fast – gone.

It bothered my husband way more than I bothered me as I soon found out. The next morning, my husband got up early and said he had to run an errand. About thirty minutes later he came back – with the mirror from the night before. I was speechless.

He told me that he noticed a car passing us right when we saw the mirror and saw the same car later in the subdivision. He thought perhaps the person scrapped. He went back to where we saw the mirror, drove around and sure enough – the person lived in the subdivision and was having a garage sale. He paid $25 for the mirror because h was determined he was getting that mirror for me.

This of course brings us to an idea. You can collect, clean and repair as needed and have garage sales.

Personally, I don't think I would scrap my local subdivision and then sell what I found to my neighbors but perhaps gathering curbside finds from other cities may be profitable.

There are some items that you may be able to sell on eBay. I'm not an eBay expert but it is an area that I am considering testing. There is also an eBay consignment shop in a neighboring town that I have been considering utilizing for a test. Then I can see how well eBay works before I take the time to set it up to do it on my own.

You also could look at the idea of selling at a flea market.

My husband and I have been selling at a local flea market for several years. What I like about flea market selling is that you work – at best – two days usually 8 hours a day and often make more money than many people make working 40 hours.

With the flea market, I work 4 to 8 hours total on the weekend but we do spend a day each week prepping the items – repairing and looking up online to see the value etc.

If this idea intrigues you, in my other book Fast Start Guide to Flea Market Selling, I go over all the things I have done including displays and signage to generate fast cash at the flea market.

There are many outlets for used merchandise that you pick up while junking.

Plus, if you are like me, you will not buy something new that you know you can get curbside.

Curbside finds can really help you out budget wise.

Just yesterday my husband picked up a generator curbside. It needed repair work and he is handy with repairing things. He had it running this afternoon – for a savings of $600 if we would have bought one new. We live just outside Chicago and the winter storms do result in power outages so this was an awesome find.

We have several riding lawnmowers – all curbside finds. All needed minor repairs, one needed a $5 part.

Scrapping and junking is great as you can make money and also find useful items – free.

Thank You

Thank you very much for buying and reading my book. I hope that you were able to gain some insight that was useful to you.

My email address is loerapublishing@hotmail.com and I would enjoy hearing from you after you start junking and scrapping or if you have questions before you begin.

We live in tough economic times and if you are one of the many, many, people who need to find extra cash flow fast – I hope that scrapping ends up being a good income source for you.

Sincerely,

Diana

P.S. – In case you wondered, the photo on the cover is one that I took of my husband. He is standing next to two of our scrap trucks and one of our small trailers is on the right.

Made in the USA
Coppell, TX
24 February 2021